I0162575

poems by

## Ronald j Palmer

# Dogged

Dogged by Ronald j Palmer

Published by POTTER'S WHEEL PUBLISHING
HOUSE
MINNEAPOLIS
MN 55378

www.POTTERSWHEELPUBLISHING.com

© 2020 RONALD J PALMER

All rights reserved. No part of this publication may
be reproduced, stored in a retrieval system, or
transmitted, in any form or in any means – by
electronic, mechanical, photocopying, recording or
otherwise – without prior written permission,
except as permitted by U.S. copyright law.

For permissions contact:
info@POTTERSWHEELPUBLISHING.com

Cover by MADURANGA NUWAN.

ISBN: 978-1-950399-02-4

ISBN: 978-1-950399-03-1 (eBook)

LCCN: 2020940106

# Table of Contents

# A Dream

At home,
no one but the dogs
and me. A quiet night.

When it nears midnight
we go out and howl
at anything that looms.

# This Dog

Foolish Husky!
My feet are cold in this draft house.
It is April, Minnesota and
Starting to snow.
She expects me to take her out
To trudge through this mess
With the holes in my boots
Along with my need for rest.
She wants to bounce down the stairs,
Down the slippery driveway
Which may cause me to fall and let her go—
A long chase that would be.

She wants to stick her nose in the fluff.
She hopes this late falling will return
The snow banks she loves to jump in.

I hope I don't have to shovel.
I want to stay dry; she looks at me and howls.
The tie-outs are rusty and may break with her pull.
If she runs down the slushy street
Animal control may find her.

If I ignore her, her revenge will be found
On the bedroom floor—
Wet socks, foul smell.

# The Wound

I don't know how it was received—
dog claw of affection?

I washed, dried and covered
with Bacitracin.

The blood spread slightly
along the back of my hand

accenting the rough dry skin.
I figure the cold Minnesota

January air will aid healing.
The rest of the day the wound

did rest on me like an emblem.

# The Retired Ref Takes A Walk

It is morning; I walk along an old football field and
spot
just beyond the end zone a number of geese
standing as if
choosing sides for a game.

(No clue where there was a football.)

Cars on the street pass me
the exhaust as harsh as angry fans.
I cannot throw a flag;
I think of players who have ignored warnings.

Looking back at the field, maybe
the geese are getting ready to honk in formation
and march a half-time show. I don't know. I am just
glad to
see that the animal kingdom can find
a use for what is left behind.

# Shilo's Ku

A husky,
second of three dogs.
On a walk,

she howls
acknowledgement to
all we pass.

Red and white,
she hopes all she greets
provide treats.

When back home,
blue eyes, mouth laughing
stolen bone.

# The Gap Between Us

In Minneapolis,
A dog in our care runs ahead of us,
Snow mists a steeple
In the dusk.
There is much I cannot tell you.

I look at the church doors
Large dark brown wood,
They do not open.
It is then I feel the gap
Between us.

You belong in the mountains,
Splinters of wood to hold up your life.
Perhaps the Rockies looking for
Peace in the whitening sky,
Among the hard rocks.

Here I belong
Watching the snow mix with dirt
The exhaust of a timid life.

You tell me
The city extinguishes us.
No one watches for forest fires
From those distant brick buildings
The dog would love to disappear among.
You say a city is a kind of wilderness
Especially here, lone wolves
Waiting, stalking at the bus stops.

I hope for a closeness
That will not exist.
A prevailing theme in my life.
The distance as unyielding
As that brick church, whose
Brownish-red walls
Stare down at us, denying entry. As if
I was asking for salvation
Without the act of what I did not have:
Prayer.

# Walking The Dogs

How lovely to hear
the sound of water tumbling
down the street drain
and to see April's
record snowfall diminish
leaving muddy grass.

# The Nature of Wisdom

A dog, in a strange house,
heads to go on the patio
not seeing the window door there.
"Dumb dog" one may say,
but isn't it a matter of perception?

A dog's perception differs from yours.
I heard a quote once, that God's wisdom
is not the wisdom of this Earth.

A philosopher would ask,
is perception intelligence?
Is "wise" knowing what is outside
what is inside?

To think deeply, you must question
the width of your own wisdom.

Hearing what my brother said,
I look at Becca as she turns away
from the door.

The only thing to do is to get up
open the door knowing
she won't jump from the patio

(and fortunately, she didn't pee).

# The Ways of Trinity

Trinity with the terrific wagging tail
A robust greeting she will not fail
Items on coffee table bound to sail
Trinity with the terrible wagging tail.

Not floppy but an almost pointed ear
She was raised with huskies, dear
At the top of the stairs she will appear
Not floppy but attentive pointed ears.

No need your arrival to announce
She is there ready to pounce
A robust greeting with every once
No need my arrival to announce.

Her howl is a police siren rhyme.
What else to say of this dog of mine
She stands so proud you could say
sublime
Half lab, half husky, listens half the time.

# A Disarray Of Crows

Was it the wind or
the barking of dogs?

A disarray of crows overhead,
a scattering of kisses

flaps in the air like wings.
The parking lot empty,

leaving me, a lone figure
embracing dusk.

# When I Awake

it is there on the blanket
on the pillow, on the chair.
Valerie swirls by
and I spy it in the air.

It appears on my shirt
on my pants
I worry if people will stare.

I find it in the kitchen
when Valerie and Trinity
glare at me hoping
for a piece of the pear
I slice for breakfast.

I must admit I no longer care
I will live with this dog hair everywhere.

# Poem for a Woman Who Walks Her Dog By My House, Daily, Sometimes We Even Chat

I started to write a poem about you
decided better not to pursue.
I have a wife, you a boyfriend
Plus, you are, at oldest, half my age.

I had a beginning but not an end,
a sentiment with no way to send.
I numbered all I could not do,
Saw it best not to write about you.

# Doggie Tonka

My dog arches her back

Legs shake, not pee this time

I am fortunate

As I have a plastic bag

Happily prepared.

# The Robins

In my neighbor's yard, the robins are dancing.
A squirrel watches in delight.
If I had a camera, I would take a picture
But instead we move on
While the robins leap around the lawn
Then fly by and perch on a nearby tree.

I look up at the nearby tree
To see if the robins are still dancing.
They leap back from tree to lawn
But refrain from the dance delight
As if the entertainment was no longer on.
With no camera, I could take no picture.

If I could capture the sight with a picture
Would we see what was in the tree
Where the robins landed on?
Would they start again dancing?
Would the squirrel again delight
To see the robins back on the lawn?

Today, there is snow on the lawn.
I suppose I could take a picture
Of the tracks in the white delight.
There are empty nests in the trees
As the wind commences its own dancing,
Its own wild show to put on?

Have the robins now moved on
Who appeared so lovely on the lawn
Leaving small signs of dancing?
Someday I will take that picture:
The robins, the squirrel and tree
I will capture the delight.

Of course there are other sights that delight
Like the dogs jumping on and on,
Or the snow dripping from a tree.
Or the racings squirrels on the lawn.
Many things that make a picture,
Many things that seem like dancing.

So take a look out on the lawn
The world may leave you a picture
Like the sights of robins dancing.

# Last Legs

So hard to watch Becca on her bad days,
I arrive home from work to find her sprawled
On the kitchen floor, unable to rise, feces
Behind her, not even trying to crawl
Too tired it seems. I manage to get her
Outside on a tie-out, and go to clean up.
After I finish, I retrieve her.
She is moving stiffly, I give her a cup
Of water.  A few steps and her nose lifts
And I wonder if it is squirrel she sniffs.
Her eyes have will to live, yet some say it's time.
To cut short or keep alive, which is the crime?
Any final verdict is delayed by her good days
She stumbles forward on her last legs.

# Becca Farewell

It seemed that day
she just wanted to nap.
She needed
much help to stand —
a minute later down
unable to rise
looking my way,
her eyes wanting rest.

Earlier that week,
her last walk —
using the high snowbanks
to stay upright.

A day before the full moon
Becca, a husky who
rarely howled, died.

In the daybreak moon
Becca's spirit shines

# April Leaving

Now, the last remnants
of snowstorms are melting
into threats of thunderstorms.

She always smiled as you passed
the house walking your dogs.

The budding has begun as the spikes
of tulips start to rip the ground.
Many greenings are starting to show.

You heard the fights from a distance
and saw that she was packing a car.

Ants have appeared on the sidewalk
a frenzy of movement.

Perhaps like the geese and the ducks
she is returning to more familiar ground.

In May, you will walk the dogs meeting one less
smile.

# A Howl Is Missing

Shilo no longer
curls in the snow,
no longer the husky smile
greets for a treat.
A decision
forced by cancer.

There is quiet now,
a howl is missing
when I walk in the door.

May the next cold snap,
the next snowfall,
bring her spirit
gently down
like flakes.

# Valerie Finds Her Fur

It is not unusual
in this warm weather
for a husky to blow
her coat.

It is not unusual
for a husky owner
to pull the loose fur
from the husky which
on a morning walk,
when Valerie stops
to sniff the grass
or bite at a tree's bark,
I do.

On the evening walk,
Valerie comes upon
a piece of her fur
I had pulled earlier
laying in the curb.
She sniffs it
as if to investigate,
to determine what dog
or animal it came from
before moving on.

I wonder if in dreams
when we come upon aspects
of ourselves, if we
recognize or must pause
in reflection. Some aspects,
I doubt, we ever come to know.

# A Brief Glimpse

Somewhere in the frozen clear
a bird chirps, then
a police siren sounds
which Trinity imitates with her howl
as if in response.

Neither the chirp nor the siren
arrives to our yard. I glance
at the repairs for which I have
neither time nor money.

Recently, I was invited to a party,
(a rare occurrence), and found
some people have happy lives.

One can see the hanging gutter,
a birch tree halfway cut down.
The night quiets and Trinity
noses to be inside. I hope
not due to disappointment.

I glance again over this yard.
Failure is simply a measurement—
I threw my rulers away long ago.
There will be time to face the losses
Wishful thinking can't prevent.

Now is time to put water in Trinity's dish.

# Another Minnesota Ending

I too could die on a day in November
where the first heavy snowfall
covers the goose poop on the sidewalk
and my dogs must be content
to sniff pee rather than taste that delicacy.
The trees offer no protection from the white
clumps hitting my silent body
nor do they tell the dogs they are free
to run past the drifts which border the park
to chase deer in the icy marsh.

Hopefully, they will be found.
Perhaps I will be found with
Shilo, Trinity and Freedom nudging
me with their noses,
Becca wondering when we will get a move on.
Or the dogs will return home a day later,
while I am left under plowed snow piles
to be discovered in Spring
with bags of dog poop, surrounded by
the start of new weeds
embracing this neighborhood.

Certainly not as poetic as some
but a different life brings a different death.
Lacking beauty, no delicate flowers await me,
Just bits and pieces of last
fall's decay, items thrown from
teen-ager filled cars, disintegrating
fast food wrappers, broken glass
from first-time liquor joyrides:
sloe gin or peppermint schnapps.

# Things People May Say When I Am Gone

He was only happy with tongue in cheek

I hear he left behind quite a mess
That happens to those
Who wait for miracles

Too bad he never found
His chips to be up

He may think he's safe
Buried in oak
But we will still call

A fellow can only
Be propped up so many times

He was pretty funny
But looks aren't everything

He didn't die
Only evaporated as if
Misery can turn to mist

Have you noticed the
Air quality has improved

Strange that no one knows
How he liked his coffee

His spirit had a spark
It showed half past
The full moon

He is in heaven
With a bag of dog biscuits
Greeted with many howls

I assumed he was trying
For some sort of
Emmitt Kelly appeal

Many times silly but
Once in a while he
Made sense, good sense

He once had grass on his yard
He once had hair on his head

There seems to be a shine
Absent from this room
A reflection missing

Ron who?

# The Dog Man

I remember seeing him
walking 'round the block.
It started with one husky;
briskly, he would go by
except when she got off leash
he moved quicker then
and with some luck
a turn in the wooded deer trail
and he'd walked back with her.

Another husky joined the walks.
This one when loose would let him
get within arm's reach
and then run off again.
His breathing seemed to get heavier,
yet by some person passing by
or a run in a fenced area
and he would be walking two huskies again.

Then a lab with pointy ears joined,
followed shortly by an American Eskimo
He tried to run with them once;
how he held onto the leash when he fell
I don't know. He walked them
daily, rain or shine, twice on weekends.

One year, the first husky was no longer there.
The man's steps were slower then.
Later, that year a husky puppy joined the group
But the elder husky disappeared soon after.

That was all years ago.
I went back to Bloomington once.
I asked if the dog man still made his rounds.
They pointed to a foreclosed house with a
condemned sign.
Said he died a few years ago. The dogs, the police
had to take away from a hysterical wife.
I remember the rain started early evening.
From my old window, I could swear
I saw him in the mist walking 5 or 6 shadowy dogs.

# Bird Gone

I found a thing with feathers
laying besides the curb
I pulled away my husky
before she mouthed the bird.

Not sure if it was some human,
car or animal that stopped its song.
We walked by later in the week
and the bird was gone.

Someone must have picked it up
thinking to leave it was a sin,
and disposed of this feathered thing
to make America great again.

# Freedom Poem
(Loosely after Eagle Poem by Joy Harjo)


To bark I warn the world
The birds, the squirrels, the postman
That this house has a watchdog.
And know I hear your car
Before it comes into view.
And there are times to
Jump joyfully:
The man coming home,
Food going into dish,
Gathering of dogs for the walk.
For I am dog exhilarated,
I bounce from floor to chair to couch
Tossing and catching
This rope in the air.
The delight you get from watching me
Is the gladness you should embrace.
You must not
Nap enough. May you let
The sorrow go. Learn release,
When you see movement outside
Let yourself bark
Let yourself bark.

# Dog Hair

Yes, I am one of those
who refer to their dogs
as their kids. They are
my girls, my care.

On Saturday mornings,
Valerie will wake me
like any child hoping
to go to the park.
Trinity like the lazy older
sister raises an eye waiting
to see if it's worth getting up.

A husky and a lab/husky mix,
they sure do like their walks
and like any parent I like hearing
a neighbor or a stranger comment
how beautiful, how well behaved they are.
Like any parent, I know how well
behaved they are sometimes not.

A person comes our way
the dogs jump towards,
Happy to meet, hoping
for a pat or a treat.

During feeding time, Valerie
will leap and twist
like a young ballerina while
Trinity will jump in excitement
like a child seeing a pile of birthday gifts.

We play tag or throw the ball around.

Then there is the dog hair
(shedding northern breed)
Vacuum cleaners wear out at our house.
Lint rollers help, but wherever I go
some strands of fur remain on my clothes.
I wear that hair like any proud father
would wear a badge made from a child's hand.

# How Appearances Are

As Valerie, (my husky) and I turn
the corner of 91$^{st}$ Street onto Russell,
what looks like a dead wren on the street
turns out to be a large brown leaf.
Valerie passes it without even a sniff
and we continue with our walk
fallen leaves looking like fallen leaves.

# Trinity's Last Day

On Trinity's last day,
I had a tooth removed
and found out an Aunt died.

On Trinity's last day
she didn't want to move
to stand her up did not work.

On Trinity's last day
her eyes shown she knew
her eyes let me know

On Trinity's last day
she laid on the vet's floor
peacefully waiting

On Trinity's last day
tears over her body
she was to wait no more.

**February/March 2020 A Poem Cycle**

# Overture

The snow spirit wanted
the vicarious thrill
of sparkling in the wind.
It didn't have the fire
but could simulate the glow.

Maybe the spirit was hoodwinked
in thinking it would matter
if it's ghostly appearance
would no longer align with fear.

Perhaps in an earlier incarnation
the spirit was snubbed causing
its reactions to be so pell-mell:
a failure of some admission test
after ghoul high school,
a phantom snub at
the specter awards.

Another burst of the wind
and the dog wants in.
I see the chill snow blown
into a shape and am reminded
once I wanted the thrill
of a sparkle as well.

# Days Before The Thaw

The chill snow was blown
into a shape as if
the diligent work of some spirit.

If the gist of this wind
was to be macabre
it was a lackluster effect.

Could one allege
that the spirit's work
was sublimated?

What can one prognosticate
by the swirl over
the evergreen?

Would the sun, if out,
cause a sparkle
in these crystals?

I can't tell
but no need to shovel
at this time.

# The Thaw Was Shortly Held

There was no need to shovel
on that foggy day a week ago.

Water was becoming
apparent, it dripped
from the gutter,
it drip in our hearts and souls
along with making an appearance
in the front hallway:
drops from our clothes.

The ice spirit would
spring back to our lives
and the wind blowing
our breath weak
would return the snow spirit.
No sculptures this time,
just places to slip.

Where do these spirits
come from? They ride
in on the winds, almost seen.
You can't say you truly believe
their presence to be more
than a trick of the eye.
But you don't deny.

The dog jumps in the air
as if to snap at them
then sticks her nose
in the snow looking
for what was lost.

She knows they don't
perform their dances for us.

# Returning Thaw

The dog knows these winter spirits
don't dance for us.
I know as well but don't trust
My instincts.

Today, the thaw is scheduled
to return and we embrace
the anticipation of 40 degrees
while other parts of the world burn.

It is bootless to search
the yard for those spirits now
or to pontificate what judgements
this early winter warming brings.

The dog with her actions tells me:
enjoy the jump, enjoy the splash,
the snow's still here
it thaws so slowly.

Worry about what
will be expunged
in a month or so.
Worries are not icicles,
they will still be there
even if turned to water.

# Unlike Icicles

Worries, unlike icicles,
remain after a thaw.
The dog digs in softened snow
for it knows what is hidden there.
You know what is hidden as well,
to think about the weather
seems more hopeful.

Whatever was coaxed
by the freeze of a spirit's breath
no longer has hold,
no longer prevents what grows.
It is a gnawing feeling
that what you tried to protect
was nothing more than a piece of bone.

# A Dissembling

The dog lays in the soften snow as if to protect
a piece of bone.

It seems the snow spirit is slipping away as the
wind
spirit brings other tidings.

We tell ourselves we are ready for happiness but
March can't be trusted.

Could a mild beginning be a bad omen?

Sadness is the stream of water
flowing down the road.

When at night the thaw freezes
at the bottom of the hill
waits misery

It will evaporate tomorrow
only to return in some other form.

# A Day In March

Misery will evaporate tomorrow
but return in another form.

The wind spirit shows it strength,
no indication of what it plans to bring.

The snow spirit last gasp can be seen
on the grass. It won't last past morning.

I wonder if these spirits know of misery;
what the snow spirit feels as his work

will be replaced by that of water.
The dog barks and gives her best husky smile

as if to say, "what do you know of misery?
Stop moping, it is time to play.

We are still alive." So I chase her
in circles around the front yard

wondering if these spirits exist at all.

# Acknowledgements:

Thanks to Cheryl Wilke for the idea for this chapbook and to the following poets who have read early versions of the manuscript: Francine Marie Toft, Alice Chu, Steve Yasgur, and Julie Adrian. I would also like to thank Cyril Mukalel, Heidi Hemmer, and Jeanne Lutz.

Also, thanks for *The Talking Stick* for publishing "Poem for a Woman Who Walks Her Dog By My House, Daily, Sometimes We Even Chat", "The Gap Between Us" and "The Retired Ref Takes A Walk".

www.ingramcontent.com/pod-product-compliance
Lightning Source LLC
Chambersburg PA
CBHW060626030426
42337CB00018B/3219